10 THINGS TO DO ON THE FABULOUS ISLAND OF PAXOS

RAY-ANNE CARR

TEN THINGS TO DO ON THE FABULOUS ISLAND OF PAXOS

ISBN: 978-1546695400

Please note that the spelling and grammar in this book are UK English.

TABLE OF CONTENTS

INTRODUCTION

In this booklet, I want to share with you some of my favourite things to do and see on the lovely Ionian island of Paxos. These include some well kept secrets based on my personal experience from many visits to this fabulous and unspoilt island.

In this second edition (updated Spring 2016) I have included walking guides on how to reach some of the popular attractions and viewpoints on foot, starting out from the main towns of Gaios, Lakka and Loggos.

It is far too easy on an island like Paxos to drive four or five km from village to village and miss out on the countryside. These additional walking guides are intended to give you a taste of the wonderful culture and flora of this stunning Ionian landscape.

Where is Paxos?

Paxos is one of the Greek Ionian Islands which hug the western coast of mainland Greece, just south of the border with Albania. The Ionian Sea separates Italy and Greece and these islands were occupied by Venetians for many centuries. The Italian legacy is clear in the architecture and cuisine of islands like Paxos and the Italians are also credited with bringing olive trees to the island.

What makes Paxos so special?

Only twelve kilometres long and four kilometres wide, Paxos is too small to have an international airport. The only access is by ferry, hydrofoil or boat from the nearby large island of Corfu, or from Parga or other ports on the mainland. This relative isolation has protected the island from mass tourism and helped retain its unique charm and tranquillity.

For an island this small, there is a wide variety of landscapes and places to explore, from the tall cliffs and crashing seas of the west coast, to the peaceful harbours and beaches of the south and east. Away from the coast, sleepy hamlets with lovely tiny churches can be reached down narrow lanes, through the landscape of small farms, olive groves and cypresses.

Most of the tourist accommodation is either in the villages of Lakka at the northern tip of the island and Loggos on the north east, or in the main town of Gaios on the East Coast. Lakka and Gaios are harbours that attract the yachts - both private and flotillas operated by tourist yachting services. A real buzz will be found in these harbours in the evenings, where the yachts have moored up for the night, with their sailors heading for the wonderful tavernas and bars. At lunchtime, Gaios harbour is visited by day trip boats from Corfu or Parga.

There are plenty of bars, restaurants and tavernas for all tastes. Whilst it can be tempting to find a favourite and revisit time after time, there are more than enough to allow you to eat in a different location for lunch and dinner over the course of a two week break, and experience the subtle differences.

The tavernas tend to be family run and it is this charm that draws visitors back year after year. If you're lucky enough to visit again and again, you will build up a list of favourite haunts, but with a couple in each of the major villages you can still get by with a different experience each day. Many are only open for the summer months.

Apart from tourism which is now the main industry, the residents of Paxos also grow olives and the local olive oil can be bought to take back home. Although there are vines on Paxos, the wine from Anti-Paxos is said to be better. This can be bought in the local bakers, in plain unlabelled bottles. Fishing boats go out most days.

The island is wonderful for walkers, and trails run from the main coast roads into the ancient olive groves and crisscross the island from east to west. This is the best way to reach many of the hidden pebble beaches and secluded coves along the 46km of coastline.

The resident population during winter is only a few thousand inhabitants, and it is remarkable that the island can accommodate all the visitors that descend every summer, without it appearing to be over-crowded.

The months of July and August are the busiest months, with a high proportion of visitors from nearby European countries. It is also the hottest, with temperatures up in the high thirties or even the low forties.

The late spring is when the colours and smells of the vegetation are at their best, and the late summer and early autumn are great for getting away for a warm break with almost guaranteed fine weather. These early and late seasons are best for walking.

There are 65 Greek Orthodox churches on Paxos and the outer islands, not including shrines. All of them have artistic and architectural details, including bell towers, remarkable hand painted frescoes and marble and inlaid features and represent some of the most interesting buildings on the island.

I do hope that you will find these short notes of the main highlights of the island interesting and are tempted to try the suggested walking routes.

Throughout this guide I may refer to a number of businesses.

I am not sponsored by any business on Paxos, and I do not receive benefits from including any references.

All errors or omissions are mine alone.

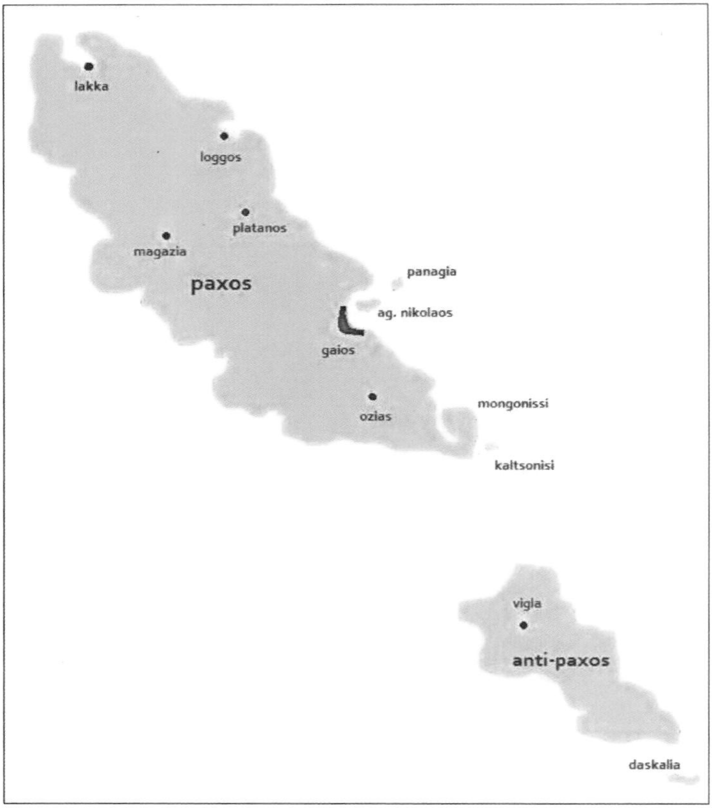

Map of Paxos and Anti-Paxos reproduced with the kind permission of the very knowledgeable team at **www.paxosinfo.com** who hold the copyright.

Additional detailed maps can be found at Google Maps.

The excellent walking guide and accompanying detailed map of all of the trails by I.K. And E. Bleasdale is available from their website - **http://www.iankbleasdale.co.uk/**

Precautions when walking in Paxos

If you do decide to walk on Paxos, you will need walking shoes or trainers.

Some paths can be overgrown with spiny vegetation and low shrubs covering rough stone and pebble tracks.

The island is basically a big volcanic mound, so any walking is going to involve some climbing, but at just under 250m above sea level at its highest, a one in four hill on any of the walks will not last more than a 100m or so.

The walks are often rough underfoot, and in some places go very close to cliff edges. Prudence is called for, especially as the island is subject to land slip.

The walk to the Tripitos Arch for example, includes walking quite near the edge of the cliffs, and this should be attempted only if the ground is dry, and the winds not too strong, and if you are confident. It will be for you to decide if the route is safe, and if you are in any doubt, it is safer to turn back than to continue.

This is not to try to deter you from some very nice walks, but over the years we have seen many examples of ill-equipped and ill-prepared walkers and those who take too casual an approach to safety.

The island has plenty of natural wildlife, most of which will seek to avoid human contact, but do watch out for the snakes. These will try to avoid you - if you are surprised by a snake, it will also be surprised by you so you should find you both head off in opposite directions. But, some of the snakes are venomous, so just be careful where you put your feet, and if you put out a steadying hand onto a tree or wall just be mindful of any animal life that might be there.

We have seen snakes even on the main roads, and on one occasion, we were surprised by one that dropped from a tree onto the path in front of us. But as expected, it made a hasty retreat.

We are told that there has not been an incident involving a snake bite on the island involving a visitor, so the risks are very low.

The far bigger risks are those of a nasty bite from some of the flying insects, so cover up or use insect repellent, especially in the evenings.

Street lights are not the norm in Paxos, especially in the villages, so I would also recommend that you bring a torch with you, plus spare batteries.

EXPLORING HISTORICAL GAIOS

Gaios (pronounced "Guy-os") is the charming capital town of Paxos. It is believed to have been named after Saint Gaius who was one of the disciples of the Apostle Paul and brought Christianity to the island.

The tomb of Saint Gaius is in the sanctuary of the church of Agios Apostili in Gaios. This church has lovely frescoes and a library and can be found just past the main car park and scooter rental as you drive into Gaios on the main road from Lakka which passes through Bogdanatika.

Gaios is the only place on the island that you can expect to find a bank and ATM, post office, pharmacy and medical services. There is also a pharmacy in Lakka during the main tourist season.

The town was built around a large horseshoe shaped bay protected by the islets of Panagia (the Virgin Mary) and Agios Nikolaos (Saint Nicholas), creating the main harbour on the island. You need special permission from the Mayor to land on these islets.

Several ferry operators run car and foot passenger services from Corfu and mainland Greece to the dock at Gaios New Port, which is also used by supply boats, water taxis and the fast hydrofoil passenger services from Corfu. Gaios New Port is only a short stroll along the quay heading north from the centre of town.

The narrow quay at the New Port end of Gaios is usually busy with yachts and fishing boats.

Between the New Port and Gaios

There is a narrow sheltered channel leading from the sea with the quay on the land side and the green forested island of Agios Nikolas on the other. On Agios Nikolas Island there are two small churches of St Nikolas and St Ioannis and a Venetian fortress dating back to 1423.

Walking from the New Port into the centre of the town, the quay becomes wider and is well served with cafes, shops and restaurants. The charm and intimate character of Gaios is immediately both appealing and welcoming.

The main square facing the harbour and the island of Agios Nikolas has the Orthodox Church of Analipsi which you cannot miss due to the red painted and curved walls. The church is often open during the day and is well worth a visit.

Gaios Town Square

This square acts as a hub for the narrow Venetian lanes which run out between three storey houses, local and tourist shops and the many bars and tavernas.

Water taxis and boats leave the quay at this point for day trips to Anti-Paxos.

There are two main supermarkets close to this square heading directly inland, together with local bakeries and a patisserie selling rich cakes. There is a local wine and olive oil shop on the harbour front, and free Wi-Fi is available at many of the bars and tavernas.

Most of the shops in Gaios are family run and offer excellent value and very friendly service. But be sure to bring coins, since loose change is always welcome.

The Folklore Museum of Paxi is situated a short stroll south along the quay from the main square and houses a wide collection of historical artefacts in what was once the primary school. The museum is not always open, so see http://www.greeka.com/Ionian/Paxi/Paxi-museums.htm.

At the end of the harbour opposite the Genesis taverna stands a landmark green statue that commemorates a local hero, George Anemoyiannis. During the Greek War of Independence in 1821 he rowed out with a lighted torch to set fire to the Turkish fleet moored at Nafpaktos. He was wounded in the attempt, captured and burnt alive. Paxiots refer to him as the “Piropolitis”, or “Citizen of Fire”.

Green Man Statue Gaios

The Genesis taverna has a Live Webcam pointing across the harbour towards Gaios town centre. You can check the weather from home on the days before you head to the island, and you can also arrange with your friends back home to stand there at a specified time, to show them the good time that you are having.

Top tips for Gaios: The Square has free Wi-Fi.

Be sure to wander around the narrow lanes and arches of the town, and experience the small hardware shops, chandlers, family run tavernas and bars which serve the mall local community. There are small intimate squares shaded by plane trees.

Look out for the Church of Agios Charalambos, the patron saint of the island, whose annual feast day is on 10 February. This beautiful church with its distinctive bell tower was built from 1875 to 1912. It is hidden away in a tiny narrow street south of the main harbour and shopping area.

Church of Agios Charalambos

VISIT THE TRIPITOS ARCH

The Tripitos Arch is a solid piece of weathered limestone which juts out into the sea on the south west coast of Paxos.

One of the best viewpoints of this eroded limestone arch is from the sea and many excursion boat trips which go around the island will pass the Arch before heading across to the island of Anti-Paxos. Motorboats can also be hired from Gaios, Lakka and Loggos, but this is not recommended if there is a strong wind forecast.

The arch can also be seen from inland. Like many of the places on the island, it is easy to park within a half kilometre or so of the site, but this would miss the fantastic countryside of Paxos.

CIRCULAR WALK FROM GAIOS TO THE TRIPITOS ARCH

This walk will take you from Gaios to the Tripitos Arch and back again. It is about 8km in length and will take about two and a half hours at a leisurely pace with a break when you get to the arch.

Head for the harbour front in Gaios and turn right.

Walk along the harbour until you reach the Genesis Taverna, opposite the green man statue. [1] Just before the

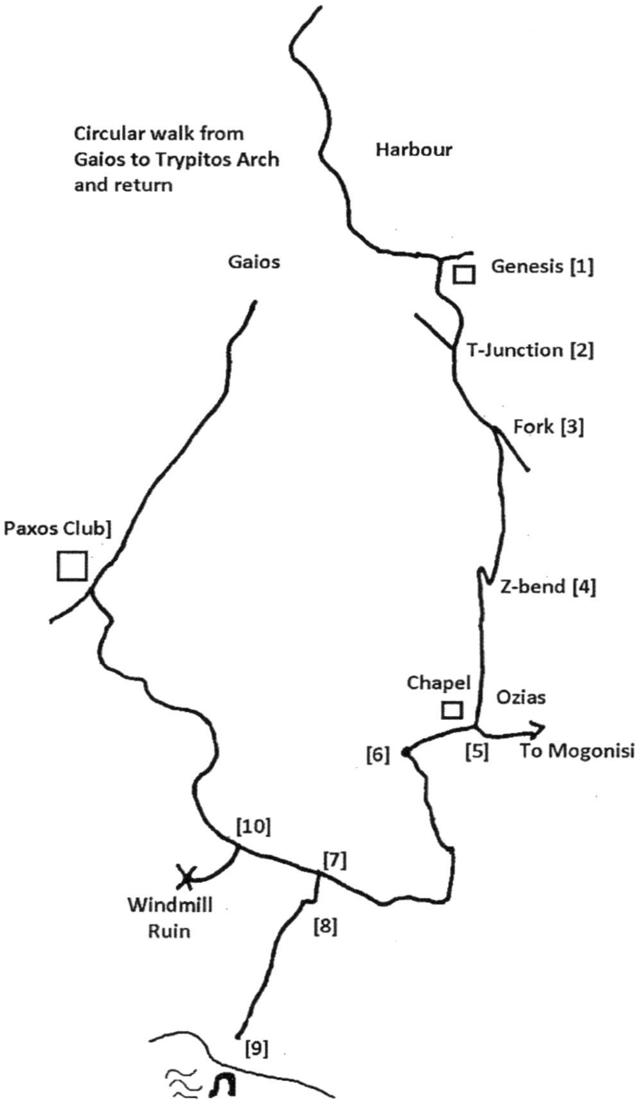
Circular walk from
Gaios to Trypitos Arch
and return
Harbour
Gaios
Genesis [1]
T-Junction [2]
Fork [3]
Paxos Club]
Z-bend [4]
Chapel
Ozias
[6]
[5]
To Mogonisi
[10]
[7]
Windmill
Ruin
[8]
[9]

Genesis taverna is a small road inland. Take this road for about 200m until you reach a T-junction where you turn left. [**2**]

From here, the walk is shaded in places by olive trees.

After 300m you arrive at a fork where you take the right hand road. [**3**] This is uphill, so slow down and take it easy.

Carry on down this road with some shade for 450m where you reach a Z bend by a chapel [**4**] and continue up the road for another 300m to a crossroads at Ozias. [**5**]

There is a small cafe facing you and a chapel on the right.

The route so far is also the start for a walk to Mogonisi, for which you would turn left, but today head right for the Tripitos Arch.

200m down the hill, just before a right hand bend, take the left turn. [**6**]

There is now a steep climb, through the woods.

After about 400m there is a hut built into the right hand wall, and 50m beyond this there is a Y-junction, take the right hand path with walls on either side.

300m further will take you to a very rough car track.

Turn left but remember this point as you will return here later. [**7**]

About 150m down the track you will reach a painted gate on the right hand side wall.

At the time of writing, this is a light green, but this could change!

Just past this gate is a narrow path heading right. [**8**]

A blue painted sign points to the Tripitos Arch.

The path is rough underfoot, and the foliage can sometimes be dense and spiny, but eventually you emerge to an excellent view of the sea.

You still cannot see the arch, but be patient as you are very close.

From this point on it is very rough underfoot, and you will see evidence that the rocks have split due to weather and earthquakes etc., and there is an ever present risk that another part of the coastline may slip into the sea.

Pick your route carefully and continue down for about 100m when the arch will come into view. **[9]**

You will see that there is a path, where the brave (or perhaps foolhardy) have walked over the arch.

Although many visitors to the island will have seen the arch from the sea, you will be in the minority; far fewer will have made the effort to see the arch from the land.

So take a breather here and enjoy the rest before your return to Gaios.

If you follow the path down to the edge, the final descent to the arch involves a lot of scrambling down quite loose limestone pebbles and should only be attempted in dry weather, and in sensible footwear.

In all cases the final one hundred metres is not for those who are not sure footed or who suffer from vertigo.

Return back the way you came, up the rocky path then the wider track until you reach the corner where you joined it. Instead of returning down the narrow path between the walls, continue left along the track.

After 200m there is a junction with a metal chain link gate and fence facing you.

To your left is a wooded area with a small shed. We have seen young goats and their parents here, climbing over the walls.

If you are still full of energy and not in a hurry to return to Gaios, you can visit the ruins of a windmill near here.

As you face the chain gate, take the narrow path just to its left, keeping the chain link fence on the right. [**10**]

This path takes you in about 200m to the ruins, where you can see the sea on both the east and west coast of Paxos.

Remember to take your bearings so that you can find this narrow path to return.

Return down the path to the track by the chain link gate and continue along the track in the direction you were heading.

Continue downhill and at each road junction take the better of the roads, until you reach a chapel.

Continue straight downwards, and follow the road until you reach a T junction opposite the Paxos Club.

Turn right and head for the centre of Gaios in about 500m.

Remember to walk on the left hand side of the road, to face the oncoming traffic.

TAKE A BOAT TRIP TO ANTIPAXOS

Many visitors to Paxos take a day trip to the tiny island of Anti-Paxos, which lies off the south east tip of Paxos.

Anti-Paxos is most famous for two things: The two stunningly pretty wide sandy beaches at Vrika and Voutoumi, which are claimed to be two of the best sandy beaches in the Ionian, and the number of vineyards which are cultivated on the gentle slopes across the centre of the island.

Passengers from boat trips and water taxi boats usually disembark on the jetty at Vrika, which has a round bay of golden sand on the foreshore and sea for swimming, bordered by pine trees and Mediterranean plants.

There are no shops on the island which has very few resident inhabitants but a small selection of bars and tavernas provide a wide variety of meals and refreshments.

Most day trippers stay all day on this beach but there is much more to explore on the rest of the island.

If you want to keep close to the sea, and avoid having to climb the cliff out of Vrika, there is a rough, but short, coastal path which curves south and links the beaches of Vrika, MesoVrika and Voutoumi if you don't mind scrambling through the spiny scrub.

A better and more enjoyable way is to walk inland from Vrika and then follow the roads down to the coastline on both the east and to the pebbly beaches on the west of the island.

It is a fairly steep climb of almost one hundred vertical metres up an unpaved pebble track to the central farmland that runs down the spine of Anti-Paxos.

The reward at the top is an excellent view over Paxos to Corfu and mainland Greece on a clear day.

The countryside is wilder than on Paxos with a carpet of wildflowers and shrubby maquis which slopes away to the south.

Take the main track that runs down the centre of the island between rows of dry stone walls. This leads through the hamlet of Vigla and then the junction with a section of tarmac road. This road winds down to the pretty and sheltered fishing harbour at Agrapidia on the east coast.

The first thing to notice is that without the heavy cover of olive trees, the landscape of Anti-Paxos is much more open with a crisscross of cobbled alley and stone terraces breaking up the heathland for farming.

If you stay on the main central track you will come to the historic church of Agios Emilianos which has 24 icons painted onto the walls.

A short distance later there is a turning to the left and a concrete path leads down to Kalouri which still has the remains of cisterns which were built to collect fresh drinking water. These were also used as a watering station by the British navy at one time.

From here you return to the main track and either carry on through the hamlet of Anthi to reach the unmanned lighthouse on the south east tip of the island, or if it is too hot or you have to return to meet your boat, retrace your steps and take the track east down to the beach at Voutoumi just after the church or walk back to Vrika.

Along the way you are never out of sight of the stunning azure blue seas which surround this isolated and tranquil island.

Top Tip for Anti-Paxos:

Many of the day trip boats and water taxis are likely to arrive around noon which is the hottest part of the day so be sure to carry lots of water and sun protection with you on this island since there are very few trees to provide natural shade.

WATCH THE SUNSET FROM THE ERIMITIS AND KASTANIDA CLIFFS

In contrast to the sheltered quiet bays along the north and east coastlines of Gaios, Loggos and Lakka, the western side of Paxos is dominated by tall limestone cliffs which rise steeply from a narrow belt of pebbly shoreline.

These western cliffs offer superb sea views and are perfect for watching the sunset over the Ocean and one of the best examples is the Emiritis cliff system and beach.

There are steep footpaths down to the beach, but the sunset is best enjoyed from the top of the cliffs and it is well worth walking or driving from Magazia to the church at Agios Apostoli on the west coast, and timing it to catch the sunset.

OPTION ONE. ENJOY THE SUNSET FROM ERIMITIS

Drive north on the Gaios to Lakka road until you pass the petrol station in Magazia.

Take a left turn down a narrow concrete track opposite the large church and follow this track until a Y-junction.

Head left signposted **Erimitis bar and restaurant**. Continue to follow these signs until you reach a car park at the bar and restaurant.

You can stop here and enjoy a cooling drink or a meal whilst watching the sunset.

If you visit the cliffs during the daytime and fancy a walk a little further, continue down the hill instead of going into the bar and restaurant and after 300m or so the concrete track ends, but there is a single path, quite rocky underfoot that will take you down to the beach.

On your way down this path, you can look left to the caves, and often you will see tourist boats moored, with swimmers enjoying the sheltered bay.

OPTION TWO. THE KASTANIDA CLIFFS

For a slightly different view, try the Kastanida cliffs and the **Sunset Taverna**.

Instead of turning left at the petrol station, continue through Magazia on the Gaios to Lakka road, and turn left just after the fire station, sign posted **Sunset Taverna and Kastanida**.

Continue for about 500m until you reach a Y-junction and turn left, again signposted Sunset Taverna.

Pass a church, a small shop and then into the olive groves.

As the road steepens downwards and bears right there is a parking spot on the left, or continue 200m further and into the car park of the Sunset Taverna.

This taverna opens in the evenings, and has a roof terrace on which you can enjoy a drink or a home-cooked meal, as you watch the sunset over the western cliffs.

If you prefer a quieter sunset, away from others, the viewing point at the top of the Kastanida cliffs is well worth a visit.

Continue (on foot) downhill from the Sunset Taverna to a T-junction.

Take the left fork in Kastanida, past a couple of houses on the right.

There are dogs that will bark at you here, doing their duty in deterring intruders - but they have always been chained up when we have passed.

The unmade track now becomes steeper and rougher.

About 300m down this track, there is a viewing point with a seat where you can see the most spectacular sunsets over the sea and cliffs. There is also a large population of nesting sea birds early in the year.

One word of warning, if you do intend to walk to watch the sunset, take a torch so you can retrace your steps safely back to the main road.

The transformation of the landscape as the sun sets over the Kastanida cliffs is worth the excursion.

MARVEL AT THE SEA CAVES OF THE WEST COAST

The geology of the islands of Paxos and Anti-Paxos is dominated by limestone and volcanic activity.

Limestone is formed from the remains of tiny shells and micro-skeletons deposited in layers on the sea bed. These layers were then compressed to form solid rock but the base chemical of all limestone is the same – calcium carbonate. This is dissolved by any acid, including acidic rain water and can be eroded by sea water, creating gaps in the rock where the limestone has been dissolved and washed away.

On the west and southern coastlines of Paxos the limestone has been broken down by waves pounding at the foot of the cliffs creating caves which are large enough for tourist boats to enter.

Some are populated by colonies of bats and seabirds, and all are best seen from the sea, so don't miss the chance to take a boat trip or hire a small motorboat from Gaios, Lakka or Loggos and explore the caves for yourself.

The sea water often appears unusually blue in the shallows.

From the sea these caves often appear as narrow slits in the limestone cliff which are just large enough for a motorboat to enter.

Larger caves can be visited by excursion boats.

DINE ON THE QUAY AT LAKKA

Lakka is the northernmost and second most inhabited village on Paxos after Gaios.

It is set in a stunning horseshoe shaped bay which creates a safe harbour for yachts and also the local fishing boats which provide the excellent selection of fresh fish which is available in the many tavernas and restaurants of Lakka.

The harbour front can be quiet or bustling when there are yachts in, and there are numerous bars, restaurants and tavernas which can be found literally at the water's edge, or a hundred meters or so inland.

On the harbour side, you can enjoy the sunshine and gentle sea breezes, and in the main square or the alleyways up towards the village bus stop, you can find more shade.

In the main square there is a taverna where you will be invited into the kitchen to examine all the dishes available, whether from the grills or from simmering pans. Here you will be spoilt for choice, but all the tavernas in Lakka provide an excellent range of dishes to suit all tastes.

Many regular visitors to Paxos prefer dining in Lakka over the crowded restaurants in Gaios during the tourist season.

If you have an apartment or villa on the island (or a yacht) then you might want to buy food to make a picnic for the beach, or even a more substantial meal - perhaps even a BBQ. Lakka has a supermarket close to the harbour front, and a little way out of the village, just after the bus stop heading south towards Magazia and Gaios, there is a butcher's shop 20m to the right of the road. Here you can buy sausages, chicken, pork souvlaki, fish - plenty of choice to test your culinary skills. The village also has a couple of excellent bakers and vegetable shops.

If you need to work up an appetite, then there are three walks I would recommend.

OPTION ONE. SHORT CIRCULAR WALK FROM LAKKA

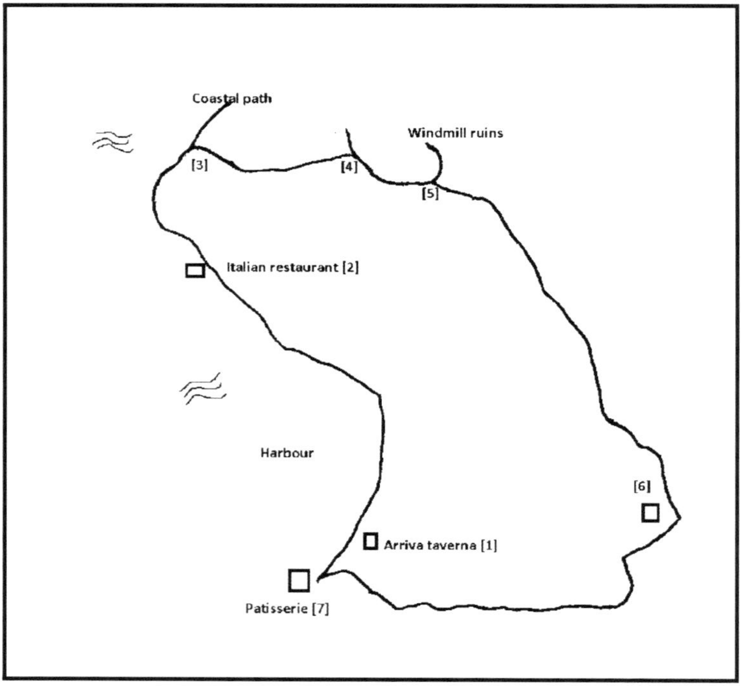

A short circular walk starting and finishing in the centre of Lakka that will take no more than 45 minutes or so, to the ruined windmill on a viewpoint.

Start on the harbour and walk in an easterly direction past the **Arriva taverna. [1]**

Then continue on the harbour path past the bars and Italian restaurant at the end of the harbour. [2]

Start to climb on the narrow path and after a house on a corner, continue until you have walked 400m in total since the Arriva taverna and take the path up to the right. [3]

This is a short steep climb past two new villas on the right. When after 150m you reach the road, turn right. [4]

Head along the road for 200m until you see a chain fence. [5]

Just to the left of the fence is a path up to the windmill ruins.

The reason why windmill ruins are worth seeking out, is that they are always built on the tops of hills to catch the wind, and this also means the views are spectacular.

To return to the centre of Lakka continue on the road, past a faux windmill [6] keeping right to pass around the side of the villa.

You will approach some gates, but just before the gates, head right downhill where there is a red and white road sign.

Continue down and to the right then into the alleyways near the apartments and villas of Lakka, ending just outside a patisserie / cafe.

OPTION TWO. MAGAZIA TO LAKKA

This is a more substantial walk starting in **Magazia, and taking in the Sunset Taverna, the Kastanida cliffs viewpoint, the Venetian house and the Lakka**

lighthouse. This walk starts in Magazia and ends in Lakka some 4km away and will take about two hours or longer.

How to get to Magazia?

The island bus travels from Gaios to Lakka at regular intervals and drops off at the turning towards Fontana in Magazia. The timetable is posted at the central bus stop in Gaios and also in Lakka.

If you park in Magazia, then at the end of the walk you would need to walk back up to Magazia to collect your car, or you can catch the local bus if you time it right, from Lakka back to Magazia.

Heading north from Gaios on the road to Lakka, pass the petrol station in Magazia on the right, and just after the fire station turn left, signposted **Sunset Taverna**.

Continue up this road for 500m to a Y-junction and head left again following the sign for the **Sunset Taverna**.

Pass a church and a small shop and a few houses, then as the road bears down and to the left then right, look for a place to park on the left.

Walk past the Sunset Taverna on your right (which is an excellent sunset viewpoint from its roof terrace) and continue to another junction where you head left.

There are dogs at the two houses on the right which will bark, but these have always been chained up when we have passed.

The road becomes a rough track, although some cars do risk it.

A short distance down this track leads to a viewpoint looking over the Kastanida cliffs. This is one of the most attractive viewpoints for watching the sunset over the Erimitis cliffs.

Continue down the track and reach a four way junction.

Take the left hand fork which heads off at a “10 o'clock” direction and head around the back end of the cliffs.

If you are visiting Paxos in the spring, the scent of the vegetation here is staggering. About 200m from the junction there is a steep track off to the left. Take this to visit windmill ruins.

NOTE – CARE NEEDED. The cliffs here are very close to the path, and there is almost continual movement of the ground, with chunks of the cliffs falling into the sea each year, so do not head too close to the cliffs (which are on the other side of a stone wall).

Return to the track and continue, bearing right in another 200m or so.

You will soon arrive at what looks like a private drive up to a house on the left. There may be a sign which directs you up this driveway to the gate.

Take this left turn - do not go straight on.

Just outside the gates for the house, there is a path between two walls on the right hand side.

Follow this slightly rough donkey path downhill until it comes out by the Venetian house at Vasilatika.

On this path, we have always trodden carefully as it would be a prime area to see snakes, we have seen only one, and it slithered away quickly on our approach.

It appears possible to walk inside the archway and around the Venetian house to a viewpoint, but spare a thought for the privacy of the occupants.

From the Venetian house head down the main track, bearing left and then right. Stay on the main track from here.

Eventually (about 1km) after passing a couple of churches at Delietatika, you will reach a fork, and the left fork is signposted to the lighthouse.

As you head down this wide gravel road you will see the lighthouse ahead, but also see a gravel road to the left.

You can follow this down to the secluded Plani beach, which is one of the few west coast beaches that can be reached on foot.

There are seldom any visitors because it is about 600m walk down, and a 600m slog back up a steep slope, and the pale gravel and white pebble beach do reflect the sun and make for a hot walk. There are no facilities for visitors on this beach.

After the beach take the road to the lighthouse. There are warning signs here that it is a naval installation, so do not head inside the gates, unless invited!

There are paths around the outside and a track down to a villa which are worth exploring.

Head back down the road away from the lighthouse and after 200m take the left turn. You walk down a track towards three holiday villas which appear to have great views of Lakka harbour.

Just before the first villa there is a narrow path, which meanders down to the Kanoni beach in Lakka, and then onwards to the south western corner of the harbour.

After this walk, you will have earned a well-deserved cool drink at any of the waterfront bars.

OPTION THREE. CIRCULAR WALK FROM MAGAZIA TO LAKKA AND RETURN VIA THE IPAPANTI CHURCH

For a longer walk, follow Option Two, enjoy lunch in Lakka and after a suitable rest, walk back up to Magazia by a different route, taking in the Ipapanti church (see **Taste Byzantine culture at the Ipapanti Church**).

TASTE BYZANTINE CULTURE AT THE IPAPANTI CHURCH

The church / monastery of Ipapanti (Ypapanti) lies in the village of Grammateika which is conveniently just off the main road between Magazia and Lakka (see directions later).

This remarkable church was built in 1600, was once the seat of a Bishop and is now the only remaining Byzantine church on Paxos.

The church itself has two domes and retains a bell tower and heraldic marks and stone doves with porthole decoration on the wall of the entrance.

The first thing to notice is the bell tower with four bells, or campanile, which is a regional landmark.

The door is sometimes open, and a circular staircase takes you up to the four bells. It may be tempting to strike the bells but please refrain out of courtesy and respect.

The church is often open either on holy days or feast days, or whilst restoration is being carried out. In the last few years there has been restoration to the murals, and latterly to the walls and roof.

If you are lucky enough to be on Paxos in May, the church is the end point of a procession of the Virgin Mary when a statue of the Virgin is carried on a bier through the towns and villages and across country to the Ipapanti church.

Local brass bands serenade the procession which is accompanied by Greek Orthodox priests carrying a blessed icon of the Virgin Mary. During and preceding the procession, flowers are strewn across the roads and paths, which is a fantastic sight in itself.

One of the interesting features of this church is that it was built in a very odd location, above a water course which means that it must be supported by extensive stone and brick foundations.

According to local lore, a shepherd found the icon of Virgin Mary Ypapantis and this was why the church was built here.

An alternative suggestion is that the church was built above the fresh water spring known locally as 'Circe's Grove' and which is still to be seen today at the foot of the foundations. In the Odysseus, the hero Ulysses was led by Nausicaa and her handmaidens to an island spring to bathe. This spring could be an ancient religious site.

Directions to the Ipapanti church

The easiest way to the church is to drive.

Coming from the car park in Lakka, head on the main road towards Magazia and Gaios and look for a turning on the right at about 1100m. There is a brown sign post for the **'Church of Ypapanti'.**

You can leave the car in a convenient place or take it (carefully) up the cement track. 700m up the hill (keep left at the junction) you come to a long house on the left.

This is the last point you can travel by car.

Turn right up the narrow track, following the directional sign, heading upwards and reach the church in about 150m.

To walk to the church from the East, you can join this walk on to a trip to the Sunset Taverna and the sunset viewpoint (see 'Watch the sunset from the Erimitis and Kastanida Cliffs').

Heading North on the Gaios to Lakka road, turn left just after the fire station signposted **Sunset Taverna**. At 500m see the sign for the sunset taverna at the Y-junction. You can head part way to the Sunset Taverna and park your car.

Return to the Y-junction and head down the road which is now on your left. This road meanders down through the trees, so there is plenty of shade.

In 800m just as the road bends hard right, there is a path heading down between two walls. Take this path, which almost immediately turns right, and after 50m turns left. The path takes you directly down to the bell tower in about 250m.

If you miss this path, do not worry, continue down the narrow road which zigzags and in about 350m you reach a long house on the right. Look for the sign post for the church on the left.

DE-STRESS IN LOGGOS

Loggos is about half way between Gaios and Lakka and the long winding narrow road down to the village meanders through pines, ancient windmill ruins and cypress trees.

Loggos is a quiet fishing village of pastel coloured two storey houses with a very picturesque harbour. Brightly coloured fishing boats bob on crystal clear water and the whole atmosphere of the village is tranquil and relaxing. Most of the tavernas, restaurants and bars are clustered around the quay where the main road through the village is reduced to a narrow strip right next to the water's edge. There is a small pebble beach to the northern edge of the village next to the ruins of a soap factory.

There is not much to do in Loggos, except sit at a bar, sipping freshly squeezed orange juice or enjoy a delicious meal, and let the day pass you by. Just what many people visit Loggos for!

Three times a day, there is a highlight as the local bus comes through the village.

The diners / drinkers at one of the restaurants must pull their chairs in, to allow room, but even so, it looks like the bus tyres have just inches to spare, and visitors all hold their breath expecting the bus to topple into the sea.

But, it is all just routine for the driver and his conductor, and you must try the bus during your stay, especially in Loggos and Lakka, where their driving skills are put to the test, with really narrow gaps.

A popular boat trip around the island of Paxos and onto the island of Anti-Paxos leaves from the jetty at Loggos and you can also hire motorboats in season.

The boat trips can be booked in advance at the bureau in the foreground of the above photograph.

On the road out of Loggos heading towards Magazia and Gaios is the lovely Levrechio Beach which is easily accessible on foot.

Other beaches such as Glyfada and Monodendri are found to the north and Marmari and Kipos to the south and all are accessible by boat or on foot.

The small car park at the beach end of the harbour is just in front of the abandoned Anemogiannis soap factory and the statue of Aphrodite still stands in place as a landmark.

CIRCULAR WALK TO THE THREE WINDMILLS AT LOGGOS

From the car park / bus stop outside the ruins of the soap factory, head around the side and back of the soap factory.

150m along the path take the steps to your left then almost immediately turn right and continue past two villas.

You will soon see the ruins of a windmill and as the path starts to bear left, look for narrow tracks on the right.

There are two tracks within metres of each other, take the second and this leads up to the windmill ruins, from where you can take in a great view of Loggos, and across the sea to Corfu.

The windmill on the hill above Loggos harbour.

Return to the track and continue in the direction you were heading before the windmill, this will take you in an anti-clockwise circuit of the headland.

After about 400m you come to a break in the wall through which you can reach the second windmill ruins.

Windmill two, on the hillside.

Be careful not to create any damage to the wall as it is not clear whether this break is intentional or not.

After comparing and contrasting the two windmills continue along the path again, and follow it around to the left.

You approach a small house - take the narrow path to the right of the house and when you reach steps, head down these back to the car park at Loggos.

The third windmill ruin is situated next to a most attractive cemetery, and can be reached by car or on foot.

By car take the road out of Loggos past the bakery and up the hill towards Fontana. At the end of a long straight, there is an olive press on the left hand side of the road (which may or may not be in operation). It has brown window frames and often a pile of crushed olives at the side waiting to be removed to be used as fertiliser or whatever other uses can be found.

Opposite the olive press there is a road with a brown signposting to **Ag Analipsi.**

Follow the road up to the right, and park opposite the cemetery.

You can walk around the windmill and capture great views of the bay.

To reach this windmill ruin on foot, again start in the car park next to the soap factory and head inland.

To the left of the supermarket there is a steep concrete road.

Head up here keeping to the main road, as it bears up and round to the right.

When the road stops just in front of two houses, take the steps and path between the houses. Ignore any side turnings and reach a slightly wider path at a T-junction, where you head left.

This is a total of 700m from the car park, and the hard climbing is over.

Continue along this track until you reach a junction with five tracks (about 200m) and take the second on the left -

I.e. the one at about "11 o'clock" position. The windmill ruins are about 150m in front of you.

To return to the Loggos car park by a slightly different route (but only if it is dry underfoot) return to the five track junction and take the second on the left (the third on the left was the one you came up).

Head down this path for 50m and take the path to your right, about 10m from the gates of a private property.

Follow this path downhill carefully, as some of the stones are covered in moss, and could be slippery. When you reach a road in about 250m turn left, and follow this down into Loggos.

Top Tip for Loggos: Try the family bakery at the end of the harbour which still uses a wood fired oven.

STROLL THROUGH THE OLIVE GROVES NEAR MAGAZIA AND PLATANOS FONTANA

Magazia and nearby Platanos are small traditional villages where social life centres around the kafeneion [the local coffee shop], the Greek Orthodox Church, the school and the small general store.

These villages in the central spine of the island seem to be immersed in an ocean of olive trees brightened by tall cypresses, pine trees and the colourful village flower gardens.

At one time the coastal villages were considered too dangerous due to frequent attacks by pirates, and Magazia was the island capital. Today it is a hamlet with two mini markets, a bakery, coffee shop, two grill rooms and the local fire station and school.

Platanos Fontana has been named after the plane tree which shades the main square close to the ancient church at the centre of the village.

These two villages are perfect for exploring the many tracks and walks that meander through the olive groves down paved and unpaved roads and traditional walled tracks and donkey trails.

The land has been worked by generations and reshaped by the building of an extensive system of stone terraces and retaining walls – and all in the local limestone.

Donkeys and mules are still used to help bring in the olive harvest. Narrow donkey and mule tracks with high dry stone walls still meander through the olive groves.

The land is dominated by the olive trees which for centuries have been the wealth of the families who manage them. It is not unusual to come across a communal olive press in a country lane and stacks of discarded olive husks outside, filling the air with a deep aroma.

The olive press on the main road to Lakka outside Magazia was built in 1865 and was still in use until 1960. It has now been restored as a museum and has a collection of traditional tools used to collect the olives, but it is not always open.

During April to June evenings these olive groves are bright with fireflies, depending on the weather.

These tracks are usually deserted and give a visitor who is willing to walk away from the coast, an incredible insight into the real character of the Ionian Islands and the culture of the people of Paxos which is firmly rooted in the landscape.

Top Tips for Magazia and Fontana

* Most of these lanes into the countryside away from the main roads are unlit at night and offer a perfect opportunity to see fireflies dancing in the olive groves if you are lucky enough to visit in the spring or early summer. So why not stop on your way back from a delicious dinner at one of the family run tavernas in Fontana or Magazia and take the time to see one of nature's finest displays for free?

* As you drive or take the local bus into Magazia on the main road from Gaios to Lakka there is a turning to the left just after the large church to the right. Only a few metres down this road you will come across an ancient heritage site. Three graves have been found which date from pre 600AD.

Follow this lane westwards through the olive groves to the lovely church of Agios Apostoli and the stunning western cliffs of Erimitis.

RELAX AND ENJOY THE NATURAL BEAUTY OF THE ISLAND

Most of the houses on Paxos have retained elements of traditional Ionian architecture which was strongly influenced by the Venetians.

Villas and town houses are rarely more than two storeys high and usually painted in soft pastel colours, with tiled roofs and wrought iron balconies.

As you walk into the countryside there are lovely examples of stone built farmhouses and windmills, storehouses and water cisterns which supported the rich culture of the olive groves, vineyards and small cottage gardens and farms.

Narrow mule tracks with dry stone walls and stone stiles crisscross the olive groves.

The beaches are mainly pebble and limestone shaded by pine trees or scrub, and are usually quiet out of the high season.

In most villages there will be a traditional white washed Greek Orthodox chapel. Some still have bell towers and many have remarkable hand painted frescoes and icons which are only seen on holy days.

The narrow village streets surrounding the harbours at Gaios and Lakka are a delight to explore.

The Ionian climate ensures an exuberance of stunning blossom and fruit trees.

For those who delight in growing beautiful roses, the Islanders seem to have no difficulty in filling their gardens with colourful displays.

And everywhere you go on the island you can be sure of a warm welcome from the local community and the many cats that help to keep the rodent population under control.

Paxos and Anti-Paxos are truly unspoilt and a delight for anyone looking for a taste of the Ionian lifestyle and culture.

I do hope that this booklet has given you some ideas on how to experience that for yourself. Have a wonderful holiday.

MORE INFORMATION ABOUT PAXOS

Please note that I have no financial interest or sponsorship from any of these companies or venues, or of any shops or tavernas mentioned in the text above and any recommendation is based on personal experience only.

General information about the island, transport and accommodation

Bleasdale Walking Map of Paxos has been a recognised guide book for walkers on Paxos. The map comes with a very detailed and illustrated Booklet describing the walks in detail plus further information about the Island.

For more information, see www.iankbleasdale.co.uk/

* http://www.foxysislandwalks.com/Paxos Walks.htm

* http://www.greece-2004.com/paxi/

*http://www.agni.gr/paxos/Walking_On_Paxos/Walking_on_Paxos/index.asp

*http://www.corfuvisit.net/default.asp?id=51&mnu=51&ACT=5&content=224&LangID=English

* http://www.paxos-greece.com/howtogettopaxos.htm

* For information on the Folklore museum in Gaios [commonly known as the Paxi Museum]: http://www.greeka.com/ionian/paxi/paxi-museums.htm

*The Erimitis Bar and Restaurant: http://www.erimitis.com

* The Sunset Taverna in Kastanida: http://www.paxosweb.gr/eating-out/Tavernas/taverna-sunset.htm

* Live-cam at the Genesis Taverna: http://www.ustream.tv/channel/paxoswebcam

Printed in Great Britain
by Amazon

58638082R00043